I0816478

MY FAVORITE DOG

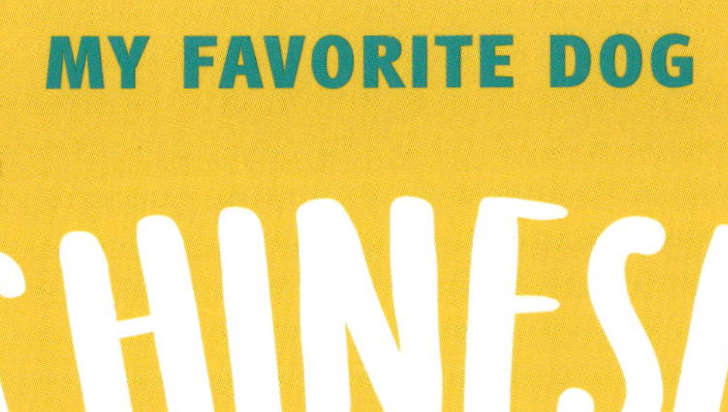

CHINESE CRESTEDS

by Renata Marie

Kaleidoscope
Minneapolis, MN

The Quest for Discovery Never Ends

This edition first published in 2022 by Kaleidoscope Publishing, Inc.

For information regarding permission, write to
Kaleidoscope Publishing, Inc.
6012 Blue Circle Drive
Minnetonka, MN 55343

Library of Congress Control Number
2021934863

ISBN
978-1-64519-465-1 (library bound)
978-1-64519-473-6 (ebook)

Printed in the United States of America.

FIND ME IF YOU CAN!

Bigfoot lurks within one of the images in this book. It's up to you to find him!

TABLE OF CONTENTS

Introduction

Sweater Weather!

Anna reaches for her favorite pink sweater, but it's not for her. It's for her dog! Daisy is a Hairless Chinese Crested. She's the perfect dog for Anna. Anna has a mild allergy to dogs, and Daisy is **hypoallergenic**.

"Playtime!" Anna yells. Daisy races to the door. She hops on her back legs and spins in circles. Anna laughs at how happy Daisy is to go outside. She loves to play outside, too. When it's cold, they both put on sweaters and head to the dog park. Anna can't wait to practice tricks with Daisy. Yesterday, she shook her hand. Maybe today she'll run up and down the seesaw!

FUN FACT

The American Kennel Club (AKC) keeps track of dog breeds. The AKC first registered Chinese Cresteds in 1991.

Chapter 1

The Story of Chinese Cresteds

A ship sails to a faraway port. A rat dashes through the kitchen. Rats can be deadly on ships. Luckily for the sailors, a Chinese Crested is hot on the rat's trail! With agility and speed, the tiny dog races after the rat. He gets closer. He catches the rat!

Chinese Cresteds like Daisy were once called Chinese Ship Dogs. They were brought on voyages to hunt ship rats. The story of Chinese Cresteds is so ancient, no one knows for sure where they came from. Some people believe Chinese Cresteds were once large African hairless dogs that were bred in China to be miniature. They soon proved to be great rat **exterminators**.

I SMELL A RAT!

Rats were feared on ships. The rodents would eat the food and spoil the cargo. They also carried diseases that could cause illness or even death. The **Black Death** was started and spread by diseased rats.

A Chihuahua

Today, Chinese Cresteds are still tiny, but they don't have to hunt rats! Dog breeds are put into groups. Chinese Cresteds are in the Toy Group. Dogs in the Toy Group are small, but they often have big personalities! A few other dogs in the Toy Group are Chihuahuas, Pugs, and Yorkshire Terriers.

FUN FACT

The World's Ugliest Dog Contest is an annual contest held in California. The Chinese Crested breed has won over 22 times and is known for being adorably ugly.

A Pug

A Yorkshire Terrier

Daisy doesn't live on a ship as her ancestors did. Thank goodness! She'd get too cold. But she still needs some exercise. Every day, Anna takes Daisy on a short walk to the dog park. Anna always puts sunscreen on Daisy. When it's cold, she dresses Daisy in a warm coat or sweater. Staying active with the right protection keeps Daisy healthy!

On their walks, Daisy always has a skip in her step and looks alert. Anna thinks she would have made a great rat hunter, but she's glad Daisy is part of her family instead. Like other Chinese Cresteds, Daisy is always excited to see the people she loves and gives them a lot of affection. Anna always feels loved by Daisy.

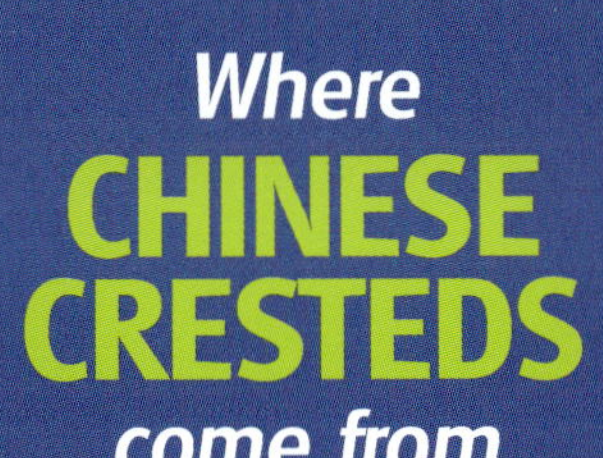

Where CHINESE CRESTEDS come from

Arctic Ocean

ASIA

EUROPE

CHINA

Pacific Ocean

AFRICA

Indian Ocean

AUSTRALIA

COUNTRY OF ORIGIN

Chapter 2

Looking at a Chinese Crested

At the dog park, Anna sneezes when other dogs get close. She notices Daisy is the only hairless dog. She loves Daisy's spunky haircut. Chinese Cresteds come in many different colors. Coat colors include black, white, chocolate, cream, and tricolor. Others are apricot, which looks like a rich, dark gold. Some Chinese Cresteds are even blue, which looks silvery gray.

A tricolor Chinese Crested

A black Chinese Crested

A white
Chinese Crested

WHAT A COAT!

With a haircut no other breed has, it's no surprise Chinese Cresteds also have unique names for their tufts of hair. The hair that grows on their heads is called a crest. The hair on their tails is called a plume. And socks of hair on their paws finish the haircut!

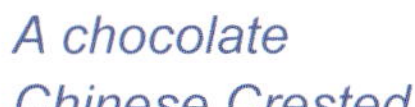

A chocolate
Chinese Crested

An apricot
Chinese Crested

THE

CHINESE CRESTED

MALES AND FEMALES

HEIGHT:*
11-13 inches (28-33 cm)

WEIGHT:
8-12 pounds (3.6-5.4 kg)

**The height of a dog is measured from the top of the shoulder, not from the top of the head.*

EARS
Large, erect
HEAD
Crest haircut,
wedge-shaped
BODY
Soft skin, fine-
boned
EYES
Almond-
shaped, set
wide apart
COAT
Hairless,
except at head,
tail, ankles,
and paws
ANKLES AND PAWS
Sock haircut

Anna points to another dog in the park. "Look, Daisy. It's another Chinese Crested." Daisy barks and trots over to say "hi," but the dog doesn't look like Daisy. He has all of his fur. Last week, Anna and her dad brought Daisy in for a checkup. The **veterinarian** told her that some Chinese Cresteds have long fur that covers their entire bodies. They're called Powderpuff Chinese Cresteds. They are not as common as Hairless Chinese Cresteds. Anna likes Daisy's haircut the best, but she couldn't wait to meet a Powderpuff Chinese Crested. *What luck!* Anna thinks as she follows Daisy to say "hi," too.

A Powderpuff Chinese Crested

Hairless and Powderpuff Chinese Cresteds look so different that they are often mistaken for different breeds.

Chapter 3

Meet a Chinese Crested!

Anna calls for Daisy. She runs up the seesaw and down to Anna. "You did it! Good girl, Daisy." Anna gives her a treat. She knows Daisy is smart, but like other Chinese Cresteds, Daisy can be stubborn. Anna has to be patient with her and use positive training.

TREAT THEM WITH KINDNESS

Chinese Cresteds don't answer well to mean words. If they are yelled at, they might not want to learn. They need to be treated with kindness and patience to grow into well-behaved dogs. Even when they make a mess.

Chinese Cresteds are surprisingly good at agility competitions. They are intelligent, and their long legs and light bodies make them elegant runners.

Anna knows Daisy will tire soon. “One more lap around the park, Daisy?” Anna asks. Daisy spins in a circle. Anna laughs, “I’ll take that as a ‘yes.’” Anna loves to watch Daisy’s **stride**. Chinese Cresteds are fine-boned and graceful. It’s no wonder Daisy runs like she’s as light as a feather. Anna knows Daisy will not run too far away. She always circles back to play with Anna.

Daisy wasn't always so affectionate with Anna. When Daisy was a puppy, it took her some time to warm up to Anna and her family. But once she did, Daisy was the most lovable pup! Like other Chinese Cresteds, Daisy is **timid** around new people but is devoted to her family.

Newborn Chinese Cresteds

Chinese Crested females can give birth to an average of one to four puppies. Chinese Crested Hairless and Powderpuff puppies can be born in the same litter.

Chapter 4

Caring for a Chinese Crested

Back home, Daisy splashes into the tub. Anna made sure the water was warm so Daisy wouldn't get too cold. Even though Daisy doesn't have a lot of hair, her skin needs cleaning. Anna gently scrubs her with the dog soap she got from the veterinarian. Then she rinses Daisy and dries her with a towel.

Chinese Cresteds can get skin irritations, allergic reactions, and sunburn. Anna always applies sunscreen to Daisy's skin before going outside. She also uses an acne lotion after bathing her.

HAIR CARE

Chinese Cresteds may not have a lot of hair, but they do need a lot of care. Their hair needs to be brushed and trimmed to keep it tidy. And they need to be washed with a gentle dog shampoo. With the right care, their hair and skin can stay clean and healthy.

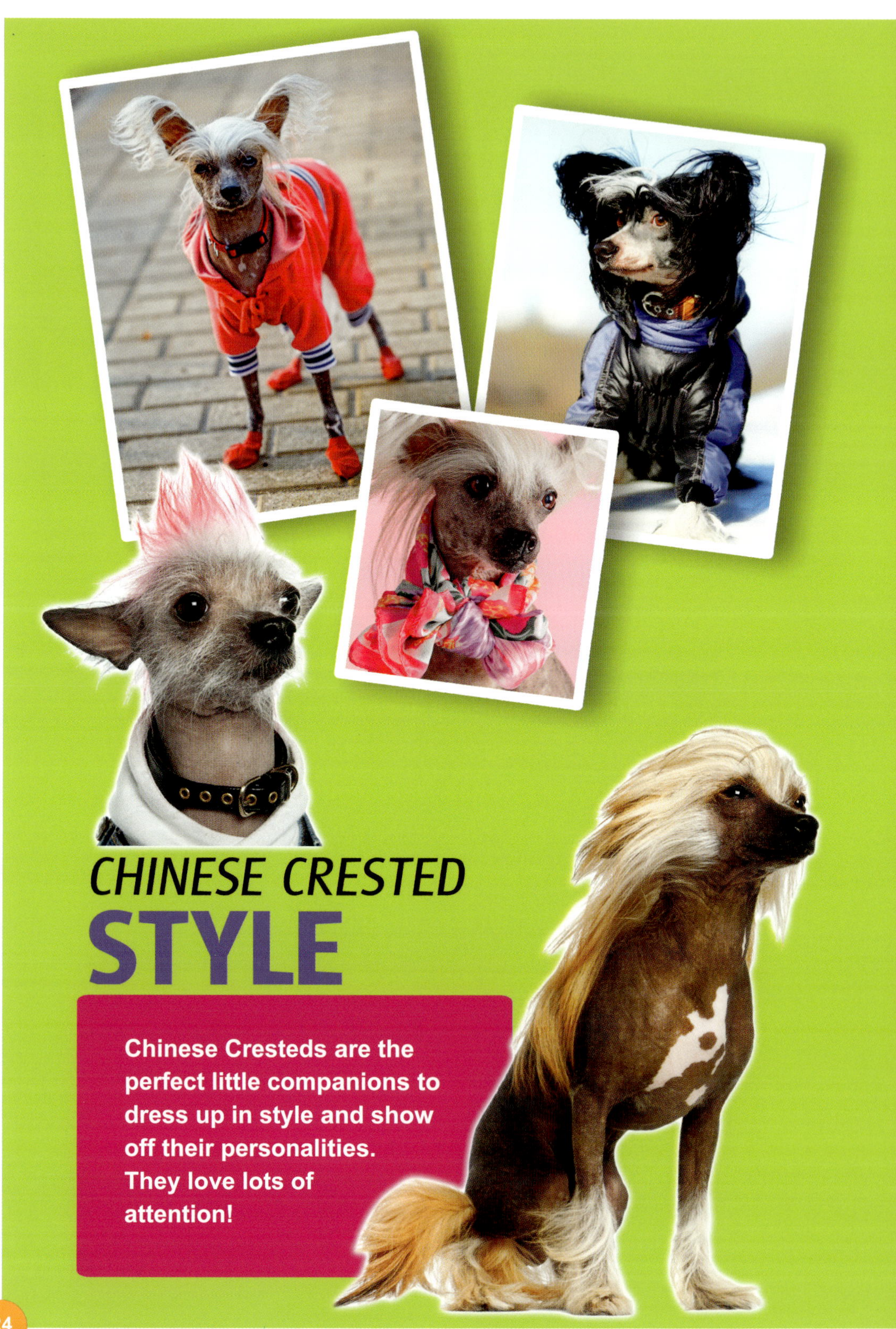

CHINESE CRESTED STYLE

Chinese Cresteds are the perfect little companions to dress up in style and show off their personalities. They love lots of attention!

FUN FACT
Like cats, Chinese Cresteds love to lounge in high places. They can be found sitting on the arm of a chair or the back of a couch.

Daisy snuggles into the couch while Anna gets her food. Daisy needs to eat the right kind of dog food to stay healthy. The vet told Anna a high-quality dog food made for Daisy's age and the Toy Group will have the **nutrients** she needs.

"Dinnertime, Daisy!" Anna calls. Daisy perks up and trots to her bowl. Anna is proud she can keep Daisy healthy.

Dogs need their teeth brushed just like humans do. After dinner, Anna cleans Daisy's teeth. She uses a special toothpaste and toothbrush made for dogs. Anna's toothpaste would make Daisy sick.

Anna takes Daisy outside one last time before going to bed. Daisy is already looking sleepy, so Anna slips under the covers and pats the bed. Daisy jumps up and cuddles right up to her to stay warm.

"Good night, Daisy," Anna says as she pets her head. She can't wait to practice new tricks with her favorite furry friend tomorrow.

After reading the book, it's time to think about what you learned. Try the following exercises to jump-start your ideas.

THINK

FIND OUT MORE. There is so much more to dig up about Chinese Cresteds. What do you want to learn? Find out more on the American Kennel Club website. Or look for a Chinese Crested club in your area. You can meet people who love them as much as you do!

CREATE

ART TIME. Can you draw a Chinese Crested? Look up a cute picture and grab some markers and paper. Will your pup have a fancy hairstyle? Will it wear a fun hat? What is its favorite toy or game? Does it have a job? The sky is the limit!

SHARE

THE MORE WHO KNOW. Share what you learned about Chinese Cresteds. Use your own words to write a paragraph. What are the main ideas of this book? What facts from the book can you use to support those ideas? Share your paragraph with a classmate. Do they have any comments or questions about Chinese Cresteds?

GROW

HELP OUT! There are dogs near you that need care. Animal shelters can be great places to volunteer and hang out with pups. Contact a shelter near you and find out if you can help. Or can your family donate food or gear to help rescue dogs? Find out why dogs end up in shelters. Is there anything you can do to help them find homes?

RESEARCH NINJA

Visit www.ninjaresearcher.com/4651 to learn how to take your research skills and book report writing to the next level!

Research

SEARCH LIKE A PRO

Learn how to use search engines to find useful websites.

FACT OR FAKE

Discover how you can tell a trusted website from an untrustworthy resource.

TEXT DETECTIVE

Explore how to zero in on the information you need most.

SHOW YOUR WORK

Research responsibly–learn how to cite sources.

Write

GET TO THE POINT

Learn how to express your main ideas.

PLAN OF ATTACK

Learn prewriting exercises and create an outline.

Further Resources

BOOKS

Mattern, Joanne. *The World's Smartest Animals*: *Dogs*. Minnetonka, Minn.: Bellwether Media, Inc., 2020.

Potts, Nikki. *Mind Benders: Totally Amazing Facts About Dogs*. North Mankato, Minn.: Capstone, 2019.

Rosen, Michael J. *A Dog's Life: Bonding with Your Dog*. Mankato, Minn.: The Creative Company, 2019.

WEBSITES

Factsurfer.com gives you a safe, fun way to find more information.

1. Go to www.factsurfer.com.
2. Enter "Chinese Cresteds" into the search box and click
3. Select your book cover to see a list of related websites.

Glossary

Black Death: the deadliest pandemic in human history. In the 14th century, it killed one out of every three people in Europe.

exterminator: a person, animal, or thing that destroys something.

hypoallergenic: something that is unlikely to create an allergic reaction.

nutrients: a substance that supports growth and health.

stride: how an animal or person walks.

timid: easily frightened or shy.

veterinarian: a doctor for animals.

Index

PHOTO CREDITS

The images in this book are reproduced through the courtesy of: Eric Isselee/Shutterstock Images, cover; Darina Matasova/Shutterstock Images, p. 1, 6; Maximillian Laschon/Shutterstock Images, p. 1 (paw prints); Medvedev Andrey/Shutterstock Images, p. 3; best animal photos/Shutterstock Images, p. 5; photolinc/Shutterstock Images, p. 7 (rat); MirasWonderland/Shutterstock Images, p. 8 (top); Eric Isselee/Shutterstock Images, p. 8 (middle); Jagodka/Shutterstock Images, p. 8 (bottom); Anna_Bondarenko/Shutterstock Images, p. 9; Abramova Kseniya/Shutterstock Images, p. 10; Josefina Lundin/Shutterstock Images, p. 12 (left); mrPliskin/iStockphoto, p. 12 (right); Eric Isselee/Shutterstock Images, p. 13 (top left); Ksenia Jihareva/Shutterstock Images, p. 13 (bottom left); Zuzule/Shutterstock Images, p. 13 (bottom right); talevr/iStockphoto, p. 14-15; Eric Isselee/Shutterstock Images, p. 16; David Raihelgauz/Shutterstock Images, p. 17 (top); Lenkadan/Shutterstock Images, p. 17 (bottom); xpixel/Shutterstock Images, p. 18 (bottom left); Eric Isselee/Shutterstock Images, p. 18; s5iztok/iStockphoto, p. 19 (top); Kseniya Abramova/Dreamstime, p. 19 (bottom); Kseniya Abramova/Dreamstime, p. 19 (bottom); Darina Matasova/Shutterstock Images, p. 20; tsik/Shutterstock Images, p. 21 (top); OlgaOvcharenko/Shutterstock Images, p. 21 (bottom); Nastasic/iStockphoto, p. 22; Sushytskyi Serhii/Dreamstime, p. 23 (top); Africa Studioi/Shutterstock Images, p. 23 (bottom); Okssi/Shutterstock Images, p. 24 (top left); Eudyptula/Shutterstock Images, p. 24 (top right); Eric Isselee/Shutterstock Images, p. 24 (middle left); RavenaJuly/Shutterstock Images, p. 24 (middle right);Eric Isselee/Shutterstock Images, p. 24 (bottom right); Natalya Antropova/Dreamstime, p. 25 (top); 279photo Studio/Shutterstock Images, p. 25 (bottom); Makidotvn/iStockphoto, p. 26 (top left); F16-ISO100/Shutterstock Images, p. 26 (top right); Subbotina Anna/Shutterstock Images, p. 26 (bottom); s-a-m/iStockphoto, p. 27; Subbotina Anna/Shutterstock Images, p. 31.

About the Author

Renata Marie is a children's book editor and author. She has also written a young adult novel and flash fiction. Renata loves sharing her stories with her mom's classroom and hanging out with her two overly curious cats and big lap dog, Takoda.